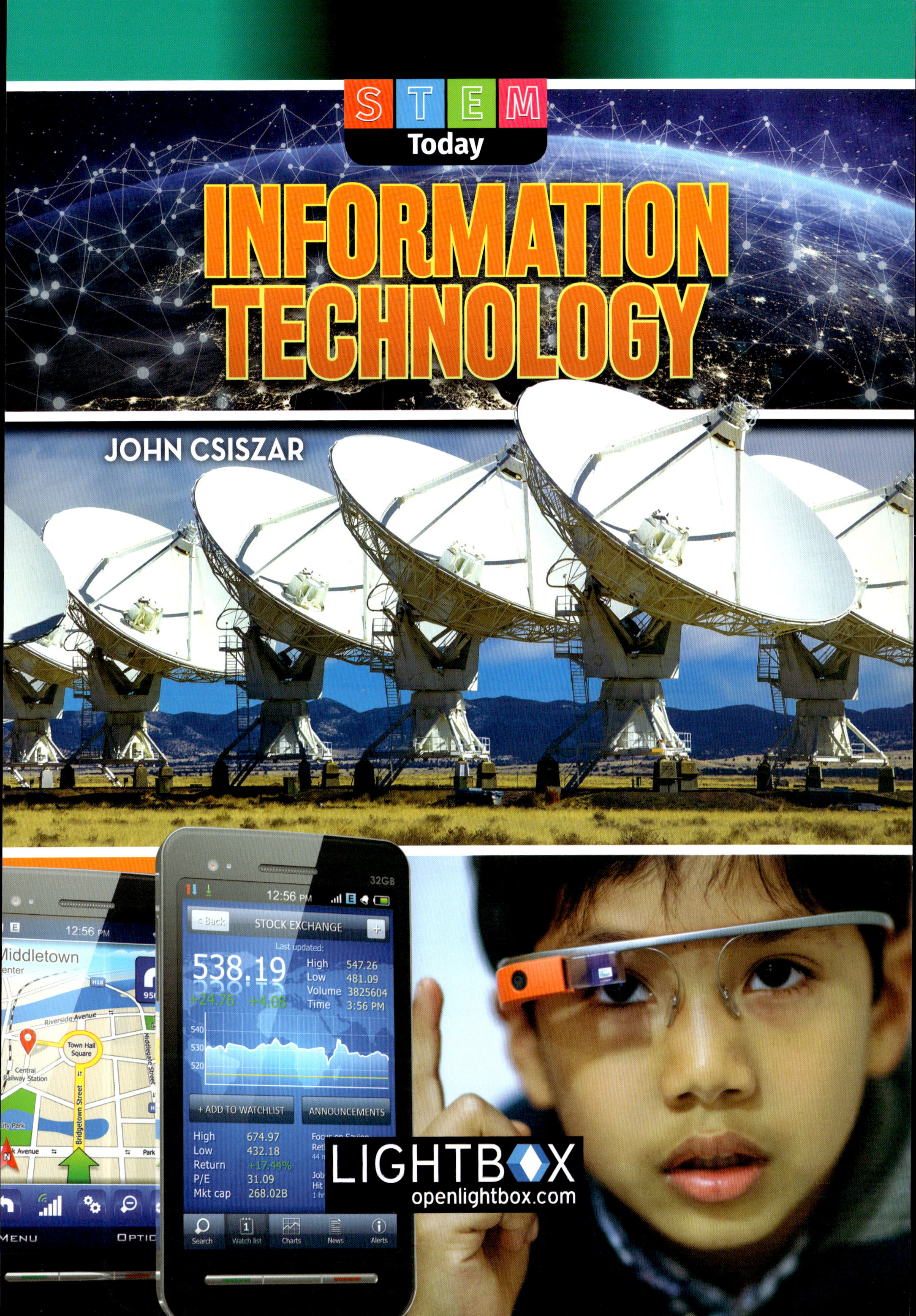

STEM
Today
INFORMATION TECHNOLOGY
JOHN CSISZAR
12:56 PM
Middletown
Riverside Avenue
Town Hall Square
Central Railway Station
Bridgetown Street
Middlegate Street
MENU
32GB
12:56 PM
< Back
STOCK EXCHANGE
Last updated:
538.19
+24.76 +4.08
High 547.26
Low 481.09
Volume 3825604
Time 3:56 PM
540
530
520
+ ADD TO WATCHLIST
ANNOUNCEMENTS
High 674.97
Low 432.18
Return +17.44%
P/E 31.09
Mkt cap 268.02B
Search
Watch list
Charts
News
Alerts
LIGHTBOX
openlightbox.com

Go to
www.openlightbox.com
and enter this book's
unique code.

ACCESS CODE

LBXH5582

Lightbox is an all-inclusive digital solution for the teaching and learning of curriculum topics in an original, groundbreaking way. Lightbox is based on National Curriculum Standards.

STANDARD FEATURES OF LIGHTBOX

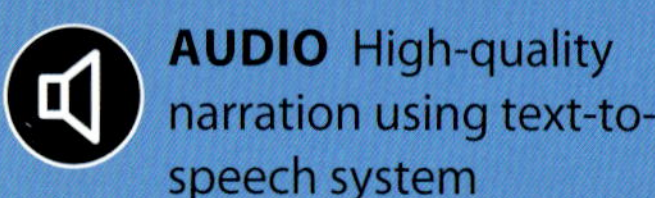
AUDIO High-quality narration using text-to-speech system

ACTIVITIES Printable PDFs that can be emailed and graded

SLIDESHOWS Pictorial overviews of key concepts

VIDEOS Embedded high-definition video clips

WEBLINKS Curated links to external, child-safe resources

TRANSPARENCIES Step-by-step layering of maps, diagrams, charts, and timelines

INTERACTIVE MAPS Interactive maps and aerial satellite imagery

QUIZZES Ten multiple choice questions that are automatically graded and emailed for teacher assessment

KEY WORDS Matching key concepts to their definitions

INFORMATION TECHNOLOGY

CONTENTS

THAT'S INFORMATION TECHNOLOGY

The field of information technology ranges from how the atoms in a computer move to how information is sent back to Earth from deep space probes.

29 percent of women have jobs in **STEM**.

African American and Hispanic women account for only **2 percent** of the jobs in computing and engineering fields.

STEM jobs are expected to grow by **18.7 percent** from **2010 to 2020**.

Modern-day society depends on storing, retrieving, and sending information so much that an entire industry, known as information technology (IT), has grown to service it. From the moment you wake up to the time you go to sleep, you probably access more information that you even realize. If you use a smartphone, surf the internet, watch television, or listen to satellite radio, you're using information technology.

Humans have always needed to acquire and share information. While the information technology industry has come a long way since mankind ran around in animal skins and took shelter under twigs and branches, in the most basic sense, society's needs have not changed much. People still want to know the latest news, find their next meal, share information with others, and understand the world around them.

As in so many other STEM (science, technology, engineering, and math) fields, innovators in information technology have transformed the world. Easy access to information for all people has educational, societal, and global benefits, from the understanding of foreign cultures and traditions to the increase in global literacy. Similarly, the ability to transmit information rapidly has wide-ranging positive outcomes. It can help create a more productive workforce or just help people keep in touch. From social media apps to smartphones with more power than the computers that ran the Moon landings, information technology touches more humans around the globe than ever before.

In 2018, more U.S. adults got news using social media than by reading newspapers for the first time.

TIMELINE

Information technology has been around since humans painted pictures on cave walls. Today's amazing inventions in IT are all built on thousands of years of human communications history.

Alessandro Volta invents the first electrical circuit.

1800

Charles Babbage introduces his Analytic Engine. This engine is considered to be the first design of a modern-day computer.

1837

1936

The first programmable computer is invented by Konrad Zuse in Germany.

1947

The transistor is invented by William Shockley, John Bardeen and Walter Brattain.

1950

The mathematician Alan Turing introduces the Turing Test. This test is a measurement of a machine's ability to reproduce human behavior.

1954

George Devol invents the first programmable robot, the Unimate.

1996

The Deep Blue supercomputer defeats world champion Garry Kasparov at chess.

2019

IBM releases the first commercial quantum computer.

1 Science and Information Technology

Invention of the Radio

Although all STEM fields play an important role in the development of information technology, inventions would have little chance of success without basic science. The scientific process of asking questions, conducting experiments, and validating results is the foundation of all technological innovation. Science helps breed this innovation because it builds knowledge over time. One scientist might have a theory, but then other scientists will make discoveries based on that theory.

All of today's methods of communication and information transfer can trace their roots back to the invention of the radio.

For example, Scottish scientist James Maxwell first suggested the existence of radio waves back in the mid-1860s. Radio waves were not proven to exist until the work of German physicist Heinrich Hertz in the late 1880s. From there, it wasn't until Italian inventor Guglielmo Marconi invented the "wireless telegraph" that humanity had truly harnessed the power of radio waves. As is the case with most world-changing technology, the simple radio technology still plays a major role in today's society. While portable radios are no longer cutting-edge technology, a device you likely use every day—your smartphone—relies on the same scientific principles discovered by early radio pioneers. When you decide to make a call, your phone sends out a radio signal and looks for a nearby cell tower. Essentially, that tower then finds the phone you're trying to call, passes along the radio signal to the tower nearest the receiving phone, and then your voice comes out the other earpiece, all courtesy of radio science.

No matter what the era, science is the driving engine behind the "gee-whiz" technology of the day. Shortly after Marconi wowed the world with his radio device, electricity was making its way through modern homes, and a vast array of consumer products was unleashed to the general public for the first time, from the telephone to the refrigerator. Transportation was on its way as well, with Henry Ford's Model A car and the Wright Brothers' first flight at Kitty Hawk both promising a new era of mobility.

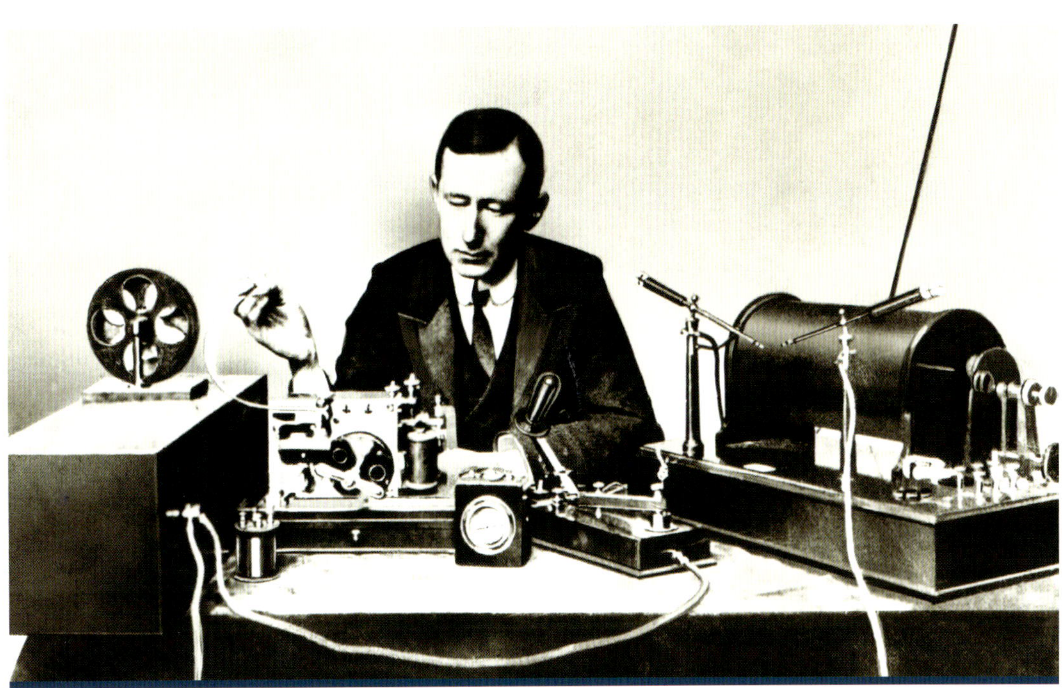

The Italian inventor Guglielmo Marconi created radio, a key forerunner to today's wireless world, in 1895.

Radio and Global Positioning Technology

What is a radio wave, and why is it so important to modern technology? A radio wave is a form of **electromagnetic radiation** that conveys information in the form of sounds or pictures. An input device, such as a microphone, converts sounds into electrical signals that are carried in wave form. When these radio waves hit a receiver, such as an antenna, they are converted back into the sounds that were transmitted. When you use your mobile phone, you speak into a microphone that converts your voice into electrical signals; these signals, in the form of radio waves, are then bounced among cell towers until they are received and converted back to the sound of your voice at the other end. That's why the sound of your voice can change when you call different people. Some phones and cell networks are better than others at transforming the received radio waves back into the sound of your voice.

Radio waves are also the core science behind Global Positioning System (GPS) technology. Most users probably don't think twice when they access an application like

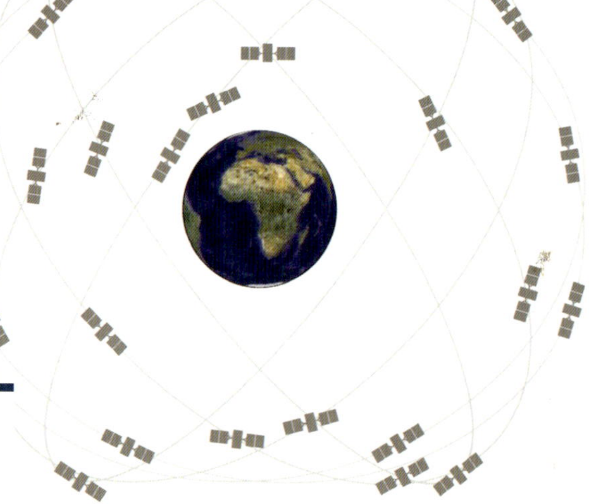

A network of satellites remains in stationary orbit around the world. The satellites network together and send location information to devices worldwide.

Google Maps. However, when you type in an address and search for directions, it's not your phone or your car that's providing the answer. It is a network of some two dozen satellites orbiting Earth that are doing the work.

Currently, the GPS system uses between 27 and 32 satellites, with some being used as backups in case of failure.

Each GPS satellite is essentially a big radio transmitter sending a signal that includes the satellite ID, orbital information, and a very precise atomic clock time stamp. A GPS receiver, such as the one in your smartphone or in your car's navigation system, processes the radio waves sent from the satellites and uses a mathematical formula to calculate the receiver's current location.

Navigation is the most obvious product of the GPS satellite network. Today, nearly every form of transport, from ships to planes to the family car, uses GPS to navigate. Beyond navigation, the applications that have sprung forth from GPS technology are mind-boggling. GPS is vital for many military uses, such as the precise targeting systems used by missiles. Geologists use GPS satellites for mapping and earthquake research. The financial services industry uses GPS time signals to help move money electronically. Hikers, cyclists, and other athletes use GPS signals to record workouts and distances traveled.

The goal of the Google Loon Balloon project is to help get internet into rural areas. Balloons are placed in the stratosphere to help build a wireless network.

Internet by Balloon

Connecting the world's computers solves some problems but doesn't address how to get information to the millions of global citizens that still can't access the internet. It may be hard to believe if you live in America, but roughly 60 percent of the world still lacks internet access. Google's Project Loon envisions getting millions of these people on the internet using helium balloons. The concept is that helium balloons can float to areas beyond the reach of cell towers. Within the balloons are solar-powered electronics that use radio waves to communicate with ground-based networks. The balloons travel through use of a balloon-within-a-balloon system. Using computer data from the U.S. National Oceanic and Atmospheric Administration (NOAA), Google can determine wind flow and direction at varying altitudes.

By inflating or deflating the small balloon inside the larger one, the system is directed to the right spot. With such technology already in place, the 4.3 billion people in the world without internet access may not be offline much longer.

Famine and Malnutrition

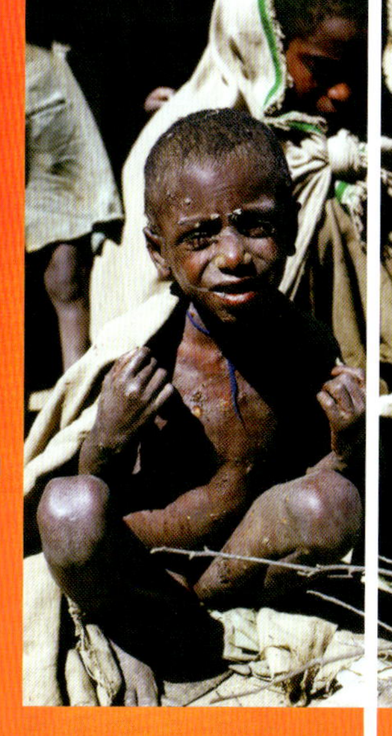

While there are lots of fun and productive ways to use your smartphone's GPS technology, scientists from the Vienna University of Technology are using it in trying to end famine. The process begins with GPS scans of Earth's surface in areas likely to have drought and famine, such as the Central African Republic. Microwave beams, which are a form of radiation like radio waves, are emitted from the GPS satellites and are used to measure the water content of soil. Scientists then couple that data with information gathered from their smartphone app called "SATIDA mCOLLECT." This app allows users in drought-prone areas to provide research data to help determine famine conditions. Information collected includes how often people eat, what the current state of malnutrition is, and whether or not people have migrated from the area or died recently.

Online Communication Advances

As big as the internet is, there are still huge amounts of important data that are not available online. Scientists in California are working to resolve that problem. David Haussler, a scientist at the University of California, Santa Cruz, is the founder of the nonprofit Global Alliance for **Genomics** and Health.

Along with the Alliance, Haussler is working on developing a **peer-to-peer network** that would allow sharing of genomic data. More than 200,000 people have already had their genomes sequenced, providing a large sample size of biomedical data. This information can be used to compare the **DNA** of sick people from around the world. With that number likely to grow into the millions, doctors and researchers will have access to a vast pool of genetic information.

For example, if you were unfortunate enough to develop cancer, your doctor would be able to run a DNA test on your tumor and compare

By gathering information from many sources, scientists are able to break down genes into large numbers of component chemicals.

it with others in the global genomic database. That could show the doctor what effect certain drugs had on others in your situation, along with the specific **mutations** involved in your tumor. Armed with this information, your doctor may be able to create a path of treatment for you. However, with this type of biomedical data not currently available on the internet, a solution is needed.

Haussler and other technical leaders at the Alliance have developed new procedures, file formats, and programming tools to help move DNA data across the internet. Their first effort was Beacon, a search engine that can access 20 publicly released databases of human genomes. With corporate Alliance members such as Google, Haussler is trying to expand this genome-focused network.

Another application of IT with DNA is the FBI CODIS database. CODIS stands for Combined DNA Index System. This FBI database contains the DNA information of wanted criminals, as well as the DNA of missing persons, from around the world.

In 1994, Congress passed the DNA Identification Act. This authorized the FBI to create a national DNA database for convicted felons, missing people, and forensic samples.

2 Technology and Information Technology

Smartphone Technology

Information technology spreads most rapidly when it translates scientific achievements into products that consumers, businesses, and governments can use. Current developments in information technology draw from both the basic scientific principles behind older inventions and from the ability of technology leaders to meet the needs of individuals and businesses. Once scientists have conceived and tested a scientific breakthrough, creators in technology fields take those proven principles and create products for the **end user** that can evolve with the times.

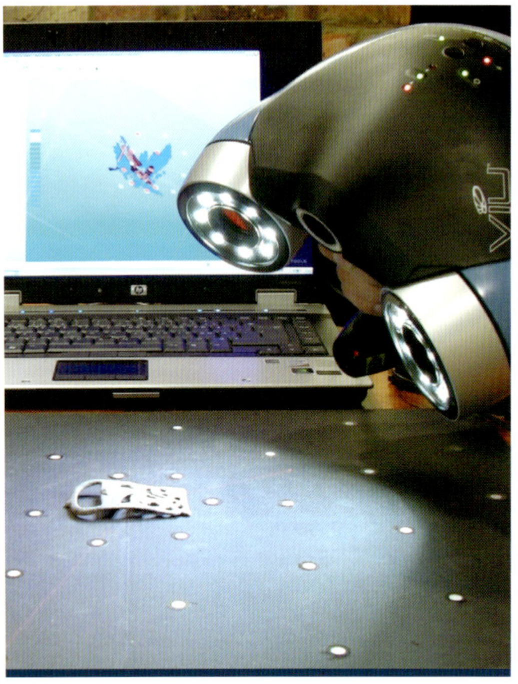
Inventors are looking for ways to put 3D scanning technology into a smartphone or tablet, which might revolutionize design and innovation.

The smartphone has come a long way from 2007, when Steve Jobs of the Apple Corporation introduced the iPhone. According to *The Economist* magazine, more than 80 percent of the adult American population will own a smartphone by 2020. Part of the reason for this growth has been the evolution of the smartphone into a multifunctional device. While the fundamental function of the smartphone still relies on radio technology, the iPhone kick-started the transformation by presenting an easy-to-use, attractive interface that combined three devices into one—an internet connectivity device, a music player with touchscreen controls, and a user-friendly mobile phone.

The adoption of the smartphone as the technological device of choice had reached the point that, as of 2015, more people searched for information using Google on a smartphone than on a computer, and more people shopped online using their devices as well.

Unbeknownst to many users, the average smartphone is already chock-full of devices and sensors that are paving the way for future innovations. For example, most smartphones already have a **gyroscope**, an **accelerometer**, and a magnetometer. These features allow your phone to know its orientation and movement. Future phones are likely to build in electrical and health sensors to detect everything from air quality to your heartbeat.

Many phones are already certified on the Miracast standard, which is essentially an **HDMI** over wi-fi connection, allowing you to project anything on one device—such as photos on your smartphone—to another compatible device, such as a television. In the future, smartphones are likely to become even more aware of their surroundings, with the ability to interact with a multitude of new devices.

3D lasers in smartphones can scan more than **10,000** points every second.

The world's first "smartphone" was invented by **IBM** in **1992**.

The term "information technology" was first used in a **1958** publication by Thomas L. Whisler and Harold J. Leavitt.

Google Glass

The ever-increasing drive to make smartphone technology more portable, convenient, and powerful led to the development of Google Glass. Released to select individuals in 2013, Google Glass is a heads-up display with the powers of a smartphone that can be worn like eyeglasses. Users can move objects in the heads-up display by utilizing a touch pad mounted on the side of the glasses. For example, using the Google Glass touch pad, you could scroll through weather reports, phone calls, text messages, or other important data, just like you would on a computer or smartphone. Google Glass is at the forefront of a new era of devices using wearable technology. By simply tilting your head or tapping the touch pad, Google Glass allows voice commands to control the system. For example, you could command your Google Glass to "call John," "take a picture," or "record a video," as Google Glass also comes with camera and high-definition video capability. For information that is read back to the user, special technology and speaker placement allow the user to hear the information without it being audible to others nearby.

Much like the apps you can download for your smartphone, Google Glass offers numerous

The clear block of plastic on the outer lens of these Google Glasses displays a constant stream of information that only the wearer can see.

The Google Glass camera captures everything the user sees, while adding layers of analysis, links, and connection. A headset button helps control functions.

software applications, with most being created by third-party developers. Some of the more interesting Google Glass apps allow for facial recognition, photo manipulation and sharing to social networks, and various exercise and travel apps. Google Glass has also proved its value in the healthcare field. As more and more health care records are stored electronically, Google Glass can access patient records and check live patient vital statistics. Google Glass has also been used by doctors to share video with other doctors during surgery.

The Google Glass program was temporarily halted in 2015 as revisions were made to the capabilities and price of the unit, which sold for $1,500 when first unveiled. The new device is expected to have numerous enhancements, including the ability to fold like a typical pair of glasses, enhanced wi-fi capability, more durability to protect against falls, and a waterproof coating. Other improvements are likely to include a faster processor, a better camera, and a bigger display.

Bluetooth Technology

Bluetooth technology is a powerful, futuristic technology that has its roots in the simple radio science of Marconi's wireless telegraph. Invented by Dr. Jaap Haartsen in the mid-1990s, Bluetooth allows for the easy, wireless connection of various devices using radio waves. Transmissions are low-cost and low-energy, and the wireless nature of radio waves often makes Bluetooth more practical than using wired devices.

For example, one of the most common uses of Bluetooth is for streaming music. With Bluetooth, you can send music from a computer or other device to a wireless speaker across the room without the need for the yards of cables and wires required by old-fashioned stereo systems.

In fewer than 20 years, Bluetooth has transformed from a simple short-distance wireless connection into the industry-standard technology behind many consumer and commercial products. Nearly all modern car manufacturers now integrate Bluetooth technology throughout their vehicles, allowing users to make calls wirelessly, send text messages, or access smartphone apps.

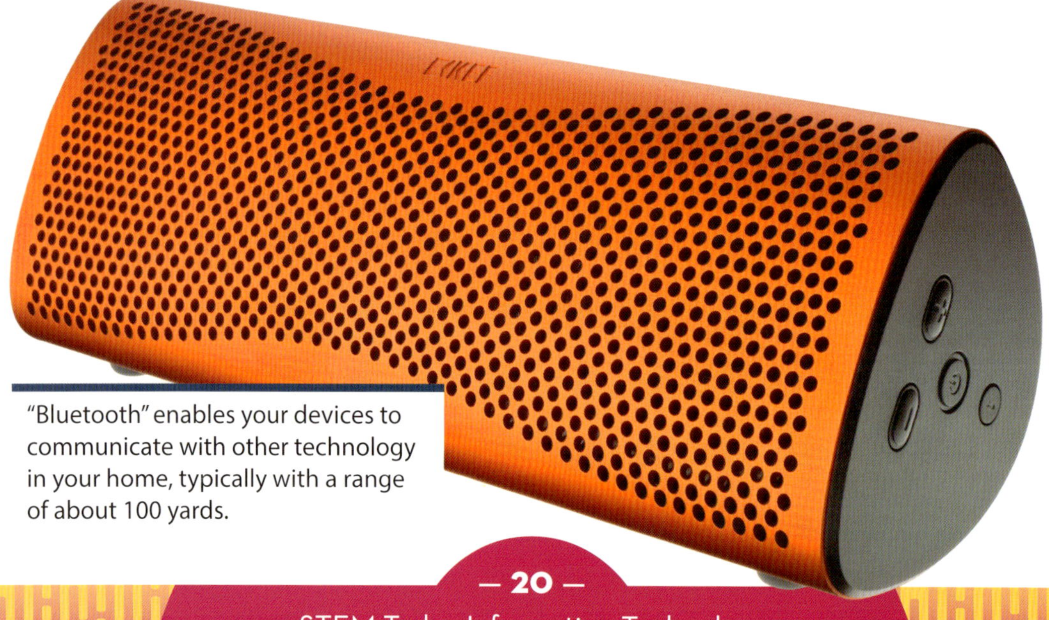

"Bluetooth" enables your devices to communicate with other technology in your home, typically with a range of about 100 yards.

The future of Bluetooth lies in complete integration with all aspects of human life. Baron Biosystems, Ltd., has developed an intelligent gear selection system that uses Bluetooth to determine the optimum gear for cyclists as they are riding. KitchBot created a Bluetooth-enabled thermometer that allows users to control slow cookers or other devices using a smartphone app. The Fliegl Tracker, a device invented by Fliegl Agratechnik GmbH, allows harvesting vehicles to communicate with one another using Bluetooth to track the complete farm-to-store cycle of grains and other foodstuffs. These and other products demonstrate how the basic science behind Bluetooth has evolved into technology that can help solve real-world problems, one at a time. But can Bluetooth grow to the point that it serves as a multi-faceted personal assistant?

Conversely, are there downsides in advancements in wireless communications like Bluetooth? With thousands of highway accidents each year, is it a win to provide a way for drivers to have calls without a phone or a loss because they have been further enabled to do something other than drive? Is it a win for all people sitting a business lunch to have instant access to communications, or a loss because the people at the lunch are not focusing on the conversations at the table? Only time will tell the answers to these questions as instant wireless communication becomes a larger and larger part of our daily lives.

MyMe Device

Israeli technology company OrCam believes that the vision of a wireless future is already here. With the development of its product MyMe, OrCam has gone one step beyond Google Glass to create a fully integrated Bluetooth assistant. Users attach a tiny, unobtrusive camera to their shirt or belt to give the MyMe its "eyes." Based on the inputs received by the camera, a computerized voice, powered by an artificial intelligence (AI), will speak via a Bluetooth earpiece to help a user analyze and interpret the world around them.

Driverless Cars

The concept of a driverless, or autonomous, car may seem like science fiction, but companies such as Google have already put self-driving cars on the road. While the reality of driverless cars dominating the roadways is still far away, the technology to pilot a car without the need for human intervention is here. Some of the biggest obstacles to the development of the autonomous vehicle have been safety and legal concerns, rather than technological difficulties.

The technology behind the driverless car works in layers. The first layer is the global positioning system. Just like a human driver needs to know where to go and how to get there, so does the driverless car. But a simple GPS system isn't enough to actually drive a car. A second layer of radars, sensors, and lasers helps an autonomous car "know" exactly where it is on a road and what hazards or obstacles are around it. A camera works as the "eye" of the car, letting it "see" where it is going. Radar serves the same function during dark or adverse conditions, such as snow or rain. Lasers operate as a circular beacon, much like a lighthouse, giving the car constantly updated scans of its surroundings.

By 2019, there have already been instances of fatalities due to driverless cars.

The third layer of technology in a driverless car is a complex set of **algorithms** that help interpret all the data that the car receives. Think about how complex the human brain is. For a car to be truly autonomous, it has to perform at that level of calculation, factoring in a multitude of variables in the blink of an eye. From the perspective of a car maker, this is perhaps the most difficult part of creating a self-driving car.

The last layer of the autonomous car is the ability to take all of the information it gathers and translate that into meaningful action, such as applying the brakes or making a turn. The computerized systems that translate such inputs already exist in most modern cars. The difference is that in current cars the input is provided by a human, whereas in autonomous cars the input will be data-driven.

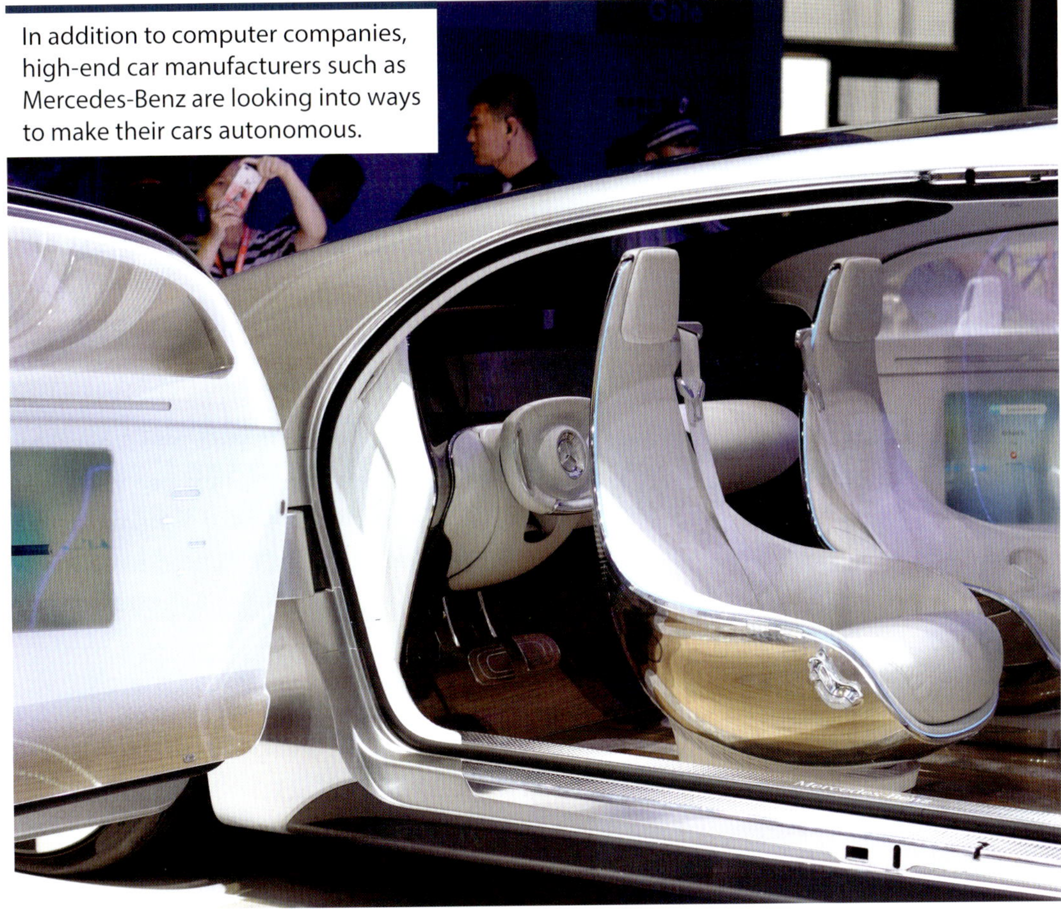

In addition to computer companies, high-end car manufacturers such as Mercedes-Benz are looking into ways to make their cars autonomous.

One idea that might be part of a driverless future is to have each vehicle broadcast a constant network of signals so that cars can actually communicate with each other.

The final push that may be needed to get self-driving cars from prototype to mass-market is real-time car-to-car communication. While radars and sensors in current vehicles can help a self-driver avoid accidents, the technology involved is very short-range and somewhat limited.

For example, a sensor may be able to detect if a car is crossing into another lane or is about to hit a vehicle directly in front of it—but what if there's a danger coming from around a corner or behind an obstacle? Vehicle-to-vehicle communication, or V2V, seeks to answer those questions by providing self-drivers with a complete picture of their surroundings.

One issue with this technology is that it is worthless unless all cars have it. A single car equipped with V2V cannot communicate with non-V2V cars. As a result, the National Highway Traffic Safety Administration (NHTSA) announced that it wanted to make V2V technology mandatory in new vehicles as soon as possible. All major car manufacturers, along with car technology companies, are currently working on adding V2V technology to all their products.

THE EFFECT OF V2V TECHNOLOGY

A pilot project conducted by the NHTSA and the University of Michigan put V2V technology into thousands of cars and tested them. The V2V technology allowed the cars to "talk" to one another by sending out information via radio wave.

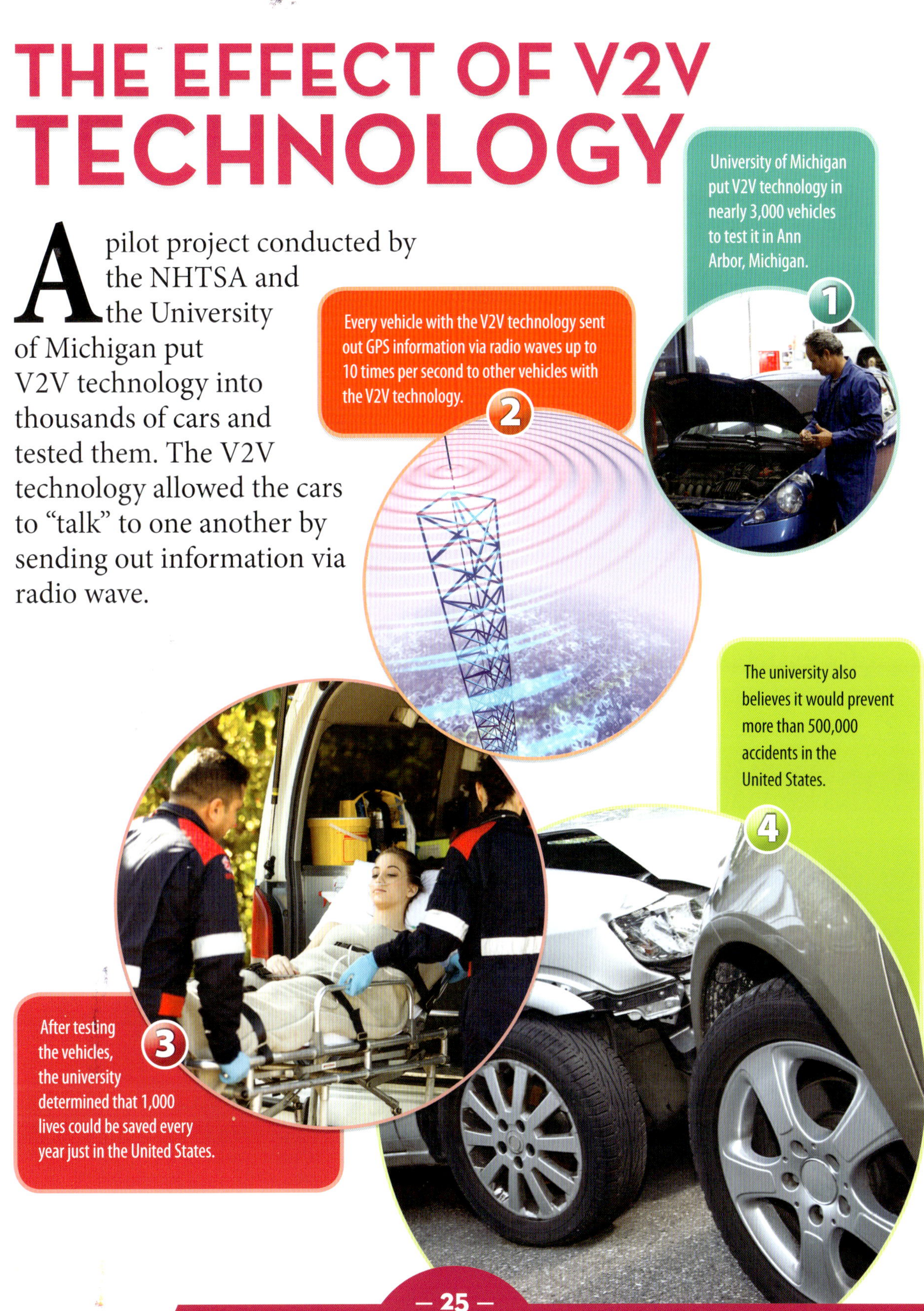

3 Engineering and Information Technology

Mobile Phone Networks and Towers

Engineering in information technology refers to how specific technical problems are solved. While radio waves might be the technological precursor of mobile phones, for example, a handset without an engineered network is useless technology. Engineers create, develop, and build the background structure that enables the use of technological devices. Sometimes, the dividing line between technology and engineering is a fine one. However, engineering generally refers to "big picture" technology, such as networks, towers, and systems, rather than smaller consumer devices, such as cell phones.

While a mobile phone's ability to transmit voice and data via radio waves is a great idea, if those radio waves don't meet up with a receiver, they'll never make it to their intended destination. Cell towers are needed to capture the

Before the invisible work of wireless networks and cell phone transmissions can happen, the hard work in steel, wire, and cable has to be done on large communications towers.

radio waves from individual mobile phones and transmit them to their recipients. Connecting cell towers and networks is an immense engineering problem for a number of reasons. Radio waves can technically pass through walls and other barriers, but the quality of the transmission deteriorates. The purpose of a tower is to rise above an area so that there's a clear line of sight with as many cell phones as possible. That reduces the risk of dropped signals or bad connections. Since towers have limited range, enough towers have to be constructed so that as a mobile phone moves out of range it easily finds a new tower to continue its connection. Well engineered towers make these switches seamless to the point that you're unlikely to know when your call has changed towers. The entire system of cell towers and switching centers is an engineering marvel—but those times may be changing.

If one inventor's idea comes to life, cell phones not only will connect people and networks, but also will provide power to each other wirelessly.

Individual mobile phones might become the next generation of cell towers. With mobile phones already being nearly omnipresent, additional towers would not have to be built if mobile phones could be engineered to receive and transmit nearby calls. Wireless telecommunications giant Qualcomm is already experimenting with technology that bypasses cell towers and allows cell phones within about 1,600 feet (500 meters) to communicate with one another. With foreign partners Deutsche Telekom and Huawei, Qualcomm conducted a test of this system, known as LTE Direct, and hopes to roll it out soon.

Batteries

Engineers are currently taking a relatively simple technology—the battery—and transforming it into a modern marvel. Batteries are essentially small-scale power plants that generate electricity using chemicals. While the chemicals and structure in modern batteries vary, most rely on the principles discovered by Italian scientist Alessandro Volta in 1800. Volta's first battery was known as the "voltaic pile," and it consisted of a stack of alternating copper and zinc discs separated by cardboard spacers soaked in salt water. Volta found that if he connected the bottom of the pile to the top with a wire, he generated an electric current.

Inside just about every electronic device you own are tiny batteries. Many of the biggest advances in technology are coming in power delivery and storage.

Today, engineering in battery technology is focused mainly on smartphones and electric cars. While the lithium-ion battery has been the standard smartphone power source for years, engineers and scientists are working on other technologies to extend the life of battery-powered devices. Scientists at the Massachusetts Institute of Technology (MIT) have been working with Samsung to develop solid-state batteries that replace the liquid electrolyte in traditional lithium-ion batteries with a solid. According to MIT, these solid-state batteries aren't flammable and can be recharged hundreds of thousands of cycles before deteriorating. Solid-state batteries also have a high energy-to-weight ratio, offering 20 to 30 percent or more of the power of a similar-sized traditional battery.

Future innovations in smartphone battery charging are right around the corner. Rice University scientists have created micro-supercapacitors by using lasers to burn electrodes into sheets of plastic. While too expensive to bring to market at this point, the resulting product could charge 50 times as fast as current batteries. Battery engineering is also moving towards nontraditional power sources. Scientists at Stanford University have developed an aluminum graphite battery that can reach full charge in just one minute. The company Prieto has developed a battery made out of a copper foam substrate. The batteries are safer, since there are no flammable components, they are fast-charging, and they carry five times the power density of the typical lithium-ion battery.

All of the advances in today's batteries can trace their roots back to the invention of the rechargeable lithium-ion battery invented in 1980 by John Goodenough.

Charging Batteries Rapidly and Cheaply

Engineers are working on even more fantastic ways to charge batteries rapidly and cheaply. Current experimental designs have been powered by radio waves, dew, sand, salt, hydrogen, solar energy, and even urine. But that's not all. The future of smartphone battery technology may be having no battery at all. Researchers at Queen Mary University of London have found a way to harness the power of sound to charge a smartphone. The scientists built a device covered with "nanogenerators" that collect sound vibrations and turn them into electrical currents.

In experiments, the developers of nanogenerators learned that traffic noise, music, and even human voices could trigger the electrical current in the phone, providing up to five volts of power.

Incredibly, electric cars have been around since 1890. It wasn't until 1997 that they were mass-produced for consumers.

In the world of electric cars, Israeli company Phinergy, in association with aluminum maker Alcoa Canada, has created an aluminum-air battery that has powered an electric car for 1,100 miles (17,70 kilometers), well above the current average. Fuji Pigment is also advancing aluminum-air batteries for cars, creating the Alfa battery with 40 times the capacity of a lithium-ion battery and boasting a unique charging device, water. When its batteries are topped off with any type of water, the battery can remain charged for up to 14 days. StoreDot, a company birthed at Tel Aviv University, is working on a charging process using amino acids to create biological semiconductors.

When completed, the company thinks it might be able to charge an electric car battery in just three minutes.

Data Storage Systems

While many parts of smartphones and personal computers are engineering marvels, data storage systems are the key to connecting modern-day devices. Before hard drives allowed you to store documents on your computer, for example, you'd have to print out anything you wanted to save. Advances in data storage technology have allowed for larger and larger storage systems at cheaper and cheaper prices, and they are far more portable to boot. It might be hard to imagine, but the world's first gigabyte-sized hard drive, produced by IBM in 1980, was housed in a cabinet the size of a refrigerator, weighed nearly 550 pounds (250 kilograms), and cost about $115,000 in today's dollars!

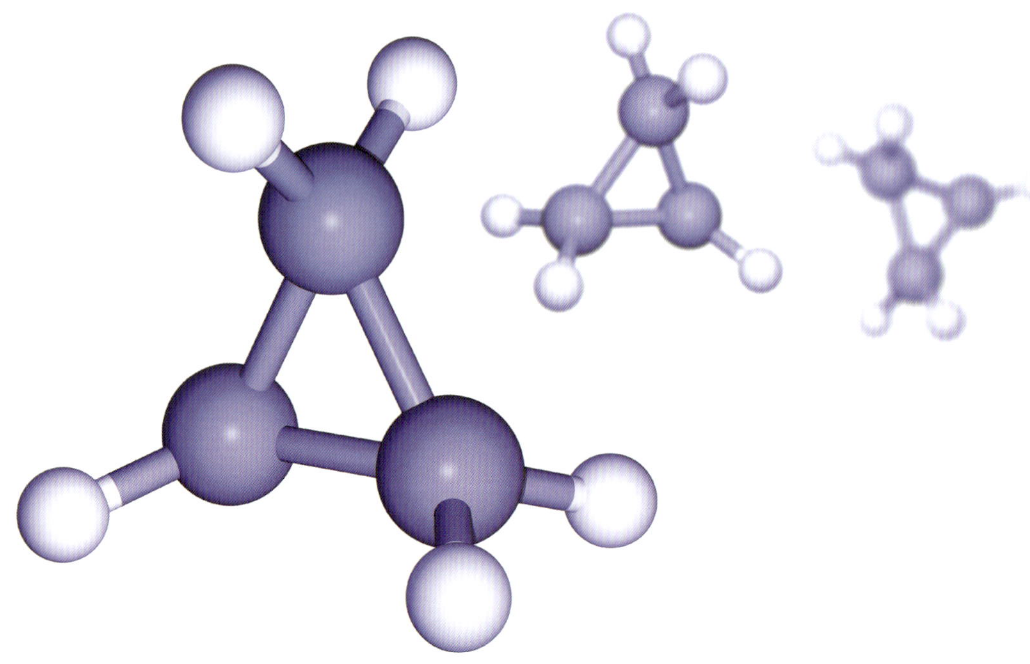

Modern data storage is so advanced that it actually relies on the behavior and positions of the atoms and molecules in the device to store the data.

By now, thumb drives like this one are almost as common as thumbs. As time has passed, they have become much cheaper and have much more storage than before.

Today, of course, you can go to any consumer electronics store, spend $90 or so and walk away with 2 or more terabytes of storage, all in the palm of your hand. Want even more portability?

Thumb drives, so called because they are about the size of your thumb, can be inserted into any USB port and can store 256 GB of data or more for less than $100. These extremely portable drives make the transfer of data between devices simple. You can copy your entire photo or music collection to a thumb drive, also known as a flash or jump drive, plug it into a computer or other device, and immediately have access to your copied files.

So What Exactly Does 3G, 4G, and LTE Mean?

When mobile phones were first developed, the original networks were only capable of sending voice calls, not data. This first generation of cellular networks was dubbed 1G. The first data transmission networks were 2G networks. While 2G networks were capable of transmitting data, speeds were often so slow that using a 2G network soon became impractical. The third generation of networks, 3G, was fast enough that users could send and receive data with reasonable speeds. The competitive nature of the mobile phone business soon led to 4G networks, also known as HSPA (High Speed Packet Access) networks, and 4G LTE (Long Term Evolution) networks. Carriers are in a furious battle to have the largest and best LTE networks, which can transmit data at up to 10 times the speed of 3G networks.

Cloud Technology

While engineering developments continue to allow smaller storage devices with larger memories, the true technological breakthroughs are occurring in the field of cloud technology.

"The cloud" is not one individual entity, but the catchy name reflects its function quite well. The cloud is a worldwide collection of servers. The engineering leap behind the cloud is that storage is moving from "hard" storage, like the hard drive in your computer or the thumb drive you carry in your pocket, to cloud storage on external servers.

As with much of the technology you use, you may not even know when you are using the cloud. Any time you save data without using the physical storage of your computer or smartphone, you are likely using the cloud.

For example, when you take a photo and upload it to Instagram, that picture is stored in the cloud. While Apple's "iCloud" storage service might give you a clue that it's a cloud-based service, if you backup your files using other services, such as Google Drive or Evernote, you're working with the cloud as well.

The idea of "cloud" storage is just another way of combining massive computing power and making it available to many users at one time.

The cloud is important to both consumers and businesses. Consumers benefit from extra storage of important data accessible from any destination. If you upload a photo or document to the cloud from your computer, for instance, you can retrieve that file from any other computer or smartphone just by logging in to your cloud account. Businesses benefit from cost savings, as they can rely on cloud servers to store their data rather than having to invest in costly on-site servers. While connecting the world seems to be done by invisible beams, at the heart of the system are hard-wired, heavily engineered machines and systems that work behind the scenes to let the information flow.

Although cloud-based storage allows for very convenient saving and sharing of files, there are also concerns about file security with so much access being available.

4 Math and Information Technology

Algorithms and Technological Development

While other disciplines are vital to the growth of information technology, math comprises the very fabric of technological development. Without the ability to calculate, scientists couldn't understand radio waves, technology manufacturers couldn't build advanced features into smartphones, and engineers couldn't develop mobile phone systems. Mathematicians create the raw data that proves that certain technologies will work. They also design the complex

Behind just about every great advance in computer and information technology is a foundation in higher math, from algorithms to set theory and more.

solutions that help keep our data safe. Advanced mathematical applications have even grown to the point where they may be able to predict the future.

Algorithms have been used for decades to help humans process and interpret data. "Algorithm" is a fancy word, but it simply refers to the steps taken or rules followed to solve a problem, typically by a computer.

Even basic algorithms, such as the steps of a recipe, typically have a mathematical component, such as "add 2/3 cup water and 1/3 cup oil."

More complex computer algorithms are built on advanced mathematics. For example, Google uses one of the world's most powerful algorithms to run PageRank, which determines how to rank web links when you conduct a search.

Amazon uses algorithms to suggest items you might be interested in purchasing, based on the products you have looked at or bought on the site.

The National Security Agency (NSA) of the U.S. government uses high-level algorithms to sift through the many bits of data it tracks from communications across the globe in its search for global threats.

Stock Market Trading

Algorithms have taken on a new importance in the world of stock market trading. By programming information such as the price of a stock, its rise or fall in price, the number of shares traded, and other factors, a trader can develop an algorithm to automatically buy or sell stocks without the need for a human. Some market players, known as high-frequency traders, use algorithms to conduct millions of transactions per day, sometimes buying and selling a stock in a few milliseconds. In fact, high-frequency trading often accounts for more than half of the entire daily volume of shares traded on the major U.S. stock exchanges.

Encryption

Encryption has been important to humanity ever since the development of the written word. The ancient Greeks and Romans used simple ciphers to transmit coded messages. "Caesar's Cipher," used by Julius Caesar, simply shifted letters to the right or left by a predetermined number, so that "A" became "D" and "F" became "I," for example. In World War II, the Germans used the Enigma machine to keep data secret from the Allies. It took a group of mathematical code-breakers to figure out the Enigma's algorithm. Today, encryption is part of the daily fabric of information technology, particularly when it comes to internet security.

Encryption methods are similar to a safe. Items inside cannot be accessed unless the safe is opened, either by a key or a combination lock. However, keys and locks are not always secure—cryptographic methods must always evolve to remain effective.

Advanced Encryption Standard, also known as AES, is a small variation on Rijndael, a highly advanced encryption algorithm created by Belgian cryptographers Vincent Rijmen and Joan Daeman. As of October 2000, it became the standard encryption method used by the U.S. government to protect vital national secrets. Essentially, AES uses high-level mathematics to break apart transmitted data into numerous pieces that are later reassembled by a code key. Without access to a key, data encrypted by AES is nearly impossible to access. However, this may not always be the case. Hackers and cybercriminals are constantly looking for weaknesses in encryption systems.

Math Fights Crime and Helps Patients

Mathematical models can be used not just to compute, but to predict. A joint study conducted by UCLA scholars and law enforcement officials managed to significantly reduce crimes rates in the Los Angeles area over a 21-month period. These results were achieved based on the creation of an algorithm using police data and mathematical research. In addition to using historical crime data to help determine the future location of serious crimes, the algorithm was programmed to "learn" as it processed new, real-time data.

The algorithm proved itself by competing against human crime analysts. In the first phase of the test, human analysts were given a map of the entire police district every day for 117 days. They were asked to indicate where crimes were most likely to occur within a specified 12-hour period. The crime-fighting algorithm managed to predict the locations of crimes more than twice as often as the human analysts.

Information to help fight crime starts its journey when police officers enter it into their in-car computer terminals.

The algorithm used had **10 years** of **police data**.

The study lasted **21 months** in Los Angeles.

The algorithm combined police data with **6 years** of **mathematical research.**

Emergency dispatch workers depend on technology to do their jobs. The math behind their work drives larger decisions, such as where to locate police stations.

In the real-world application of the study, police officers were dispatched on random days to patrol areas selected by either the human analysts or the algorithm. As in the first phase of the study, the mathematical algorithm resulted in the reduction of more than twice as many crimes as the human analysts.

The test was blind, meaning neither the patrol officers nor their commanders knew whether their orders came from a human analyst or the computer algorithm.

In addition to lowering crime, the study suggested that the use of the predictive mathematical algorithm could save Los Angeles $9 million per year in court, victim, and societal costs.

Researchers at the University of Illinois at Chicago have stretched the boundary of what a predictive mathematical algorithm can do by creating one that can interpret what you intended to do and taking its own corrective action. For example, stroke patients often have to struggle against their own bodies to complete certain tasks. The algorithm developed in Chicago seeks to overcome that problem by analyzing a person's actions and determining their intention.

The study hopes that the algorithm can power what it dubs a "psychic robot," or a machine that helps complete a task calculated to be the original owner's intent. In the case of the stroke patient, this could translate into a prosthetic that helps reduce or eliminate shakes or tremors if a patient is intending to move in a straight line. In 2019, there are already hands and other limbs that are designed to help people with body tremors. Just one of these inventions is a hand stabilizer that allows people with debilitating tremors to feed themselves.

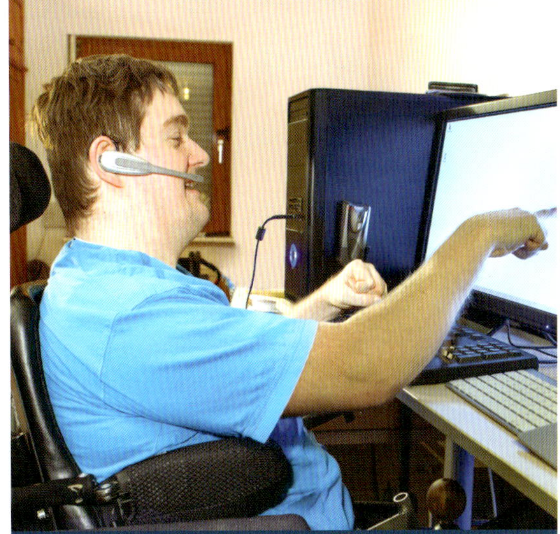

Technology has been a huge help to many disabled people. New ideas are using high-end math to create ways for more human-computer interaction.

Other Applications

The algorithm developed in Chicago could also be plugged into a car's electronics to help steer the car in accordance with the driver's wishes. For example, if you're driving in a straight line down a road but suddenly slip on a patch of ice, the algorithm may be able to help the car correct its path and return it as soon as possible to its intended straight-line path.

STEM AND INFORMATION TECHNOLOGY AROUND THE WORLD

Information technology has made the world a very small place. Today, we can have instant video conferencing between 20 people who are all sitting in different countries. Each day, our ability to share information gets faster and faster.

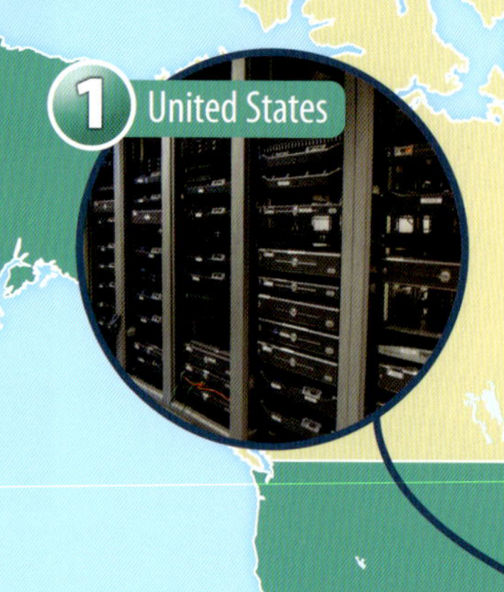

North Pacific Ocean

North Atlantic Ocean

South Pacific Ocean

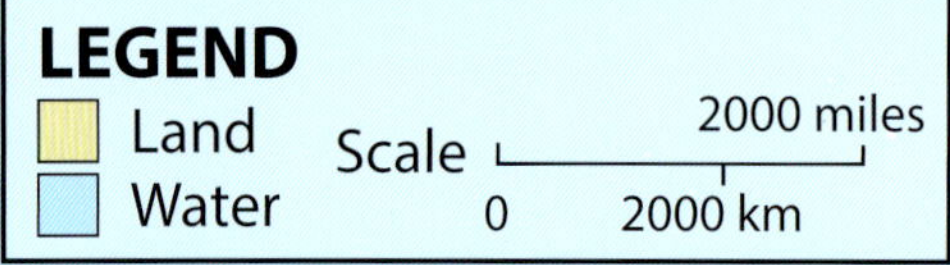

1 United States

The world's fastest supercomputer is located at the Oak Ridge National Laboratory (ORNL) in Oak Ridge, Tennessee. It was made by IBM and can perform 200,000 trillion calculations per second.

2 Australia

Wi-Fi was invented in Australia by the physicist John O'Sullivan. This was the first time that computers could communicate without being wired together. He patented his idea in Sydney, Australia in 1992 and then again in the United States in 1996.

Indian Ocean

South Atlantic Ocean

③ Great Britain

The Enigma Machine was an encrypting device that was used extensively by the Germans during World War II. The Enigma codes allowed for secure communications during the war. They were finally broken by Alan Turing's team of mathematicians at Bletchley Park in Buckinghamshire, England.

④ China

The Chinese Academy of Sciences, headquartered in Beijing, have begun the research required to create the first "quantum satellite." Once built, this satellite will allow quantum communications between Earth and space. This new technology will increase the security of transmissions all over the world.

RESEARCH PROJECTS

Science

1. Find statistics comparing the rate of internet usage and also how many people have access to it in the United States compared to other countries around the world.
2. Create a chart or graph showing the results of your research.

Engineering

1. Visit the websites of cellular service providers to pull up maps of their LTE coverage in the United States.
2. Determine which network has the most extensive coverage.
3. Use research in the library or online to determine why this might be the case.

Technology

1. Search the internet and corporate websites of Mercedes-Benz and Audi.
2. Determine when they anticipate having fully automated cars available for sale to the public.
3. Using the information available online, create a list of possible events or developments that could slow down or speed up this schedule.

Math

1. Find a website explaining how to use "Caesar's Cipher".
2. Translate a written sentence into a coded version.

QUIZ to Take

1

How many people have already had their genomes sequenced?

2

What are two products that make use of Bluetooth technology?

3

What is the main function of V2V technology?

4

Name the Italian inventor of the radio.

5

Which is the faster network, 3G or LTE?

6

How does math-based encryption help solve privacy issues?

7

What is an algorithm?

8

What form of electromagnetic radiation carries both mobile phone calls and global positioning satellite signals?

9

What is another name for a driverless car?

10

What is the "cloud"?

ANSWERS

1 More than 200,000 **2** Cars and wireless speakers **3** Communication between vehicles **4** Guglielmo Marconi **5** LTE **6** It breaks apart transmitted data and reassembles it with a key **7** A set of rules or instructions **8** Radio waves **9** An autonomous car **10** A worldwide collection of servers

KEY WORDS

accelerometer: an instrument used for measuring acceleration

algorithms: sets of rules or instructions, typically used in computer programming

DNA: deoxyribonucleic acid, the carrier of genetic information in nearly all living organisms

electromagnetic radiation: waves containing electric and magnetic fields that carry energy at the speed of light

end user: the individual actually using a product

genomics: study of the complete set of genes in organisms

gyroscope: a mechanical device using a rotating wheel to aid in navigation

HDMI: a standard for connecting high-definition video devices

mutations: genes in a living things with altered structures, resulting in changes that may be transmitted to future generations

peer-to-peer network: decentralized computer network in which all computers have equal status and responsibilities

INDEX

LIGHTBOX

SUPPLEMENTARY RESOURCES

Click on the plus icon found in the bottom left corner of each spread to open additional teacher resources.

- Download and print the book's quizzes and activities
- Access curriculum correlations
- Explore additional web applications that enhance the Lightbox experience

LIGHTBOX DIGITAL TITLES
Packed full of integrated media

VIDEOS

INTERACTIVE MAPS

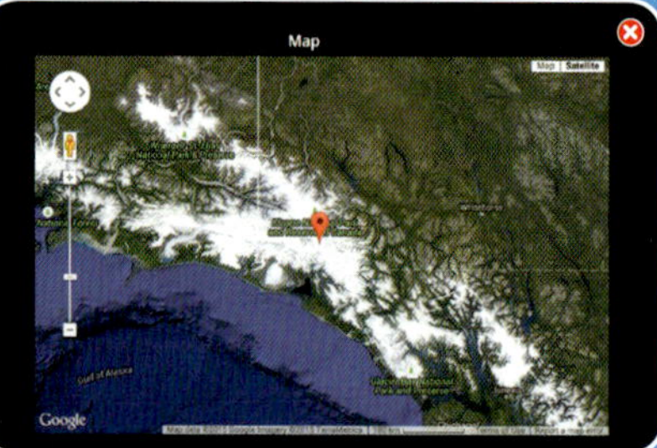

WEBLINKS

SLIDESHOWS

QUIZZES

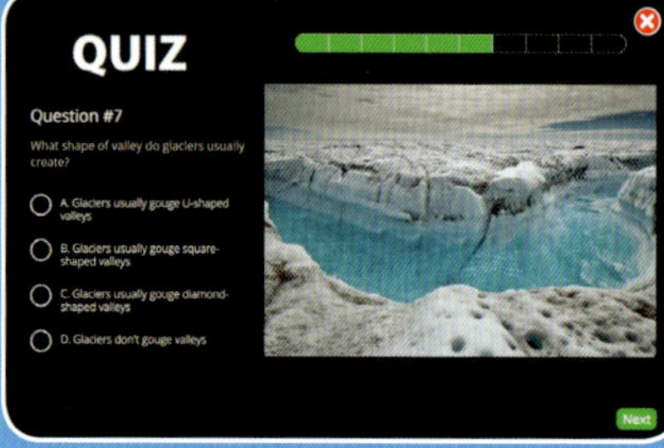

OPTIMIZED FOR

- ✔ TABLETS
- ✔ WHITEBOARDS
- ✔ COMPUTERS
- ✔ AND MUCH MORE!

Published by Smartbook Media Inc.
350 5th Avenue, 59th Floor
New York, NY 10118
Website: www.openlightbox.com

Library of Congress Control Number: 2019939912

ISBN 978-1-5105-4473-4 (hardcover)
ISBN 978-1-5105-4474-1 (multi-user eBook)

Printed in Guangzhou, China
1 2 3 4 5 6 7 8 9 0 23 22 21 20 19

062019
121218

Project Coordinator: John Willis
Art Director: Terry Paulhus

Photo Credits
Every reasonable effort has been made to trace ownership and to obtain permission to reprint copyright material. The publisher would be pleased to have any errors or omissions brought to its attention so that they may be corrected in subsequent printings.

The publisher acknowledges Alamy, Dreamstime, Getty Images, and Wikimedia as its primary image suppliers for this title.

First published in 2017 by Mason Crest.